www.jkboyer.com

J. K. Boyer

ROARING
MOUSE

a fun and exciting illustrated children's bedtime story
Early Reader Book

Roaring Mouse
Copyright © 2016 by James K. Boyer

Suddensuccess, LLC
600 Riverplace Suite 6648
Detroit, MI 48207
United States

www.jkboyer.com

ISBN-13: 978-1533417367
ISBN-10: 1533417369

❦

For my children: Sophia, Brittany, and Colin who are braver and stronger than they know. And most of all for my loving wife, Birgit, who is the center of the best part of my life.

In the heat of the Sonoran desert, the daytime belongs to animals well adapted to life under the giant cacti that give Arizona's Saguaro National Park its name. Animals like jackrabbits, vultures, roadrunners, horned lizards, and Gila monsters all have unique traits and behaviors that help them to thrive in the desert heat.

At the end of the day the desert air cools as the sun sets over the park. The big animals slip away into the shadows of the giant prickly plants. The nighttime belongs to the small animals that come out in the cool darkness of the desert night to find their food.

Alison, a southern grasshopper mouse is out hunting beetles. She is a mommy. Her small family is safely underground in their nearby burrow waiting for her.

Anubis, a deadly Arizona bark scorpion is also out hunting beetles tonight. His venom is so dangerous that it can even kill a person.

If these two small hunters meet one another tonight, there will be a fierce battle under the light of the rising moon. This has been the way between mice and scorpions for more than a thousand generations.

From the shadow of a rock beneath a giant cactus, Alison sees Anubis on the path before her. She holds perfectly still; even her sensitive whiskers are motionless. She sniffs the air between them and listens intently for the sounds of any other animals that might enter the fray. She knows that Anubis will raid her burrow and take her pups if given the chance. She *will not* give him that chance.

  The beetle that she was hunting is forgotten as it scurries away to safety. All that matters is the coming battle for survival. She knows that only one of them will see the morning come and that the other's story will end here tonight.

Anubis is not surprised when he sees
Alison in the shadows. He knew that she
was there before either hunter could see
the other. He knows the world around him
through so much more than just his eyes.
His eight legs are so sensitive to the
vibrations in the ground that he can feel
the sand shifting under the weight of the
beetle as the insect scurries away from the
two hunters toward safety.

At the end of his tail, curled above his head, Anubis carries the ancient weapon of his species. His sting brings burning pain, paralysis, and death. He has killed much bigger things than Alison before. He *is* the thing in the darkness that other animals, even humans, fear. If she faces him in battle, he *will* sting her.

Their arena is a small patch of cold, open ground awash in a pool of white moonlight beneath the cloudless night sky. They circle each other cautiously and then suddenly Alison lunges for Anubis. Her tiny jaws snap shut on empty air as he slips deftly beneath her attack while his deadly sting flashes down toward her face from his tail arching up and high above her. She closes her eyes and darts swiftly to one side, her sensitive whiskers brushed by his tail alert her to his stabbing counter attack.

Alison pivots, vaults, and somersaults away from him— but too slowly. She lands hard on her left side. She paws at the fierce burning of Anubis' venom in her face and shoulder where he has already stung her twice. She rebounds to her feet and faces him once more. He whirls to face her again and raises his tail, ready to sting.

But, there is another name for the tiny southern grasshopper mouse; the Native American people of the southwestern U.S. call it the "scorpion mouse."

The burning in Alison's face and limbs goes cold but not numb as Anubis' venom within her is changed by her body. She is *not* paralysed. She no longer feels pain. *She* holds the advantage in the generations long arms race between these tiny predators. She attacks again— seizing and flinging Anubis about by one of his claws. She pounds him again and again against the desert floor and then pounces upon him ending the fight with a powerful bite.

Panting. Shivering. Overcome by the sudden stillness of the silence after her fury— Alison rises up on her hind legs and throws back her tiny head. She roars her victory howl wild and loud at the full moon shining brightly in the cloudless night sky above her.

The battle is done. Alison makes her way back home through the cool, quiet, sweet smelling air of the desert night. She finds her family waiting safely for her in their burrow among the rocks beneath the beautiful night blossoming flowers of a giant Saguaro cactus. ∎

The End

The Science behind the Story

Scorpions are members of the class Arachnida. That means that they are closely related to spiders, mites, and ticks. There are almost 2,000 scorpion species in the world today but only about 40 varieties have strong enough venom to kill a person. The Arizona bark scorpion (*Centruroides sculpturatus*) is the most dangerous scorpion in North America. It's found in the Sonoran Desert including Arizona's Saguaro National Park. The scorpion's venom contains a powerful neurotoxin that causes terrible pain in humans and most other mammals when stung.

Arizona bark scorpions sting about 200 people each year. A sting can cause sharp pain, tingling, swelling, numbness, dizziness, shortness of breath, muscular convulsions, involuntary eye movements, coughing, and vomiting. Three (3) human deaths have been attributed to the Arizona bark scorpion in the United States since the year 2000.

But, the southern grasshopper mouse (*Onychomys torridus*) is an extremely ferocious and capable hunter, staking out and defending up to twenty-five acres of territory. Unlike other mice, it's exclusively carnivorous. It eats the beetles, and grasshoppers of the Sonoran Desert. That's how it gets its name. And, unusually for an animal this small— the southern grasshopper mouse hunts and eats venomous scorpions and centipedes.

The southern grasshopper mouse has special amino acid variants present in its nerve cells that bind the venom's peptides transforming the scorpion's neurotoxic venom into a pain killer. After the first couple of stings, the neurotoxin doesn't cause the mouse any pain. Instead it has the opposite effect, blocking pain signals instead of transmitting them, temporarily turning off the mouse's sense of pain, and sending the tiny hunter into a frenzied "beast mode." After winning a battle or defending their territory, southern grasshopper mice rear up onto their hind legs and triumphantly howl like wolves! ■

About the Author

Best selling author J. K. Boyer was born and raised in Detroit, Michigan. He lives with his wife and their three children in Zürich, Switzerland. A graduate of Wayne State University in Detroit, he teaches Business Analysis throughout Europe and the Middle East. His passions include parenting, fitness, investing, and martial arts. He is a member of Mensa, appreciates good design, enjoys speaking before any sized audience, and is older than he looks. ∎

www.jkboyer.com

Link to Detailed Scientific Research

http://www.ncbi.nlm.nih.gov/pmc/articles/PMC4172297/

www.ingramcontent.com/pod-product-compliance
Lightning Source LLC
Chambersburg PA
CBHW040308010626
45792CB00025B/1478